W9-AXA-257

Lex: 960

AFRICAN AMERICAN CULTURE

BY CATHERINE NICHOLS

Rourke
Publishing LLC
Vero Beach, Florida 32964

Developed by Nancy Hall, Inc., for Rourke Publishing.
© 2006 Nancy Hall, Inc.

Acknowledgments are listed on page 48.

All rights reserved. No part of this book may be reproduced or utilized in any
form or by any means, electronic or mechanical, including photocopying, recording,
or by any information storage and retrieval without permission in writing from the publisher.

www.rourkepublishing.com

Photo research by L. C. Casterline
Design by Atif Toor and Iram Khandwala

Library of Congress Cataloging-In-Publication Data

Nichols, Catherine.
  African-American culture / by Catherine Nichols.
    p. cm. -- (Discovering the arts)
  ISBN 1-59515-517-1 (hardcover)
  1. African American arts--Juvenile literature. I. Title. II. Series.
  NX512.3.A35N53 2006
  704.03'96073--dc22

                            2005010730

Title page: *Jazz Singers*, ca. 1934, by Archibald J. Motley, Jr.
Jazz and blues music inspired many painters, including Motley,
who created lively scenes of Chicago's nightlife.

Printed in the USA
10 9 8 7 6 5 4 3 2 1

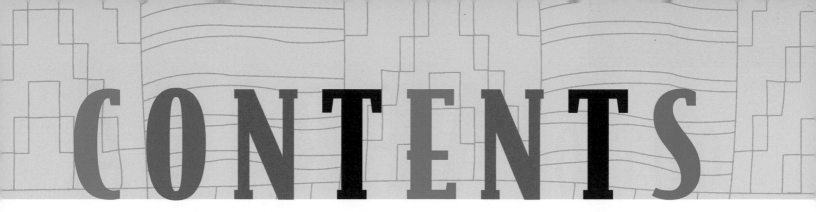

CONTENTS

OUT OF AFRICA

Africans came to the New World in chains. They left behind their homes, their belongings, and their culture. Or did they? Although they could not carry anything with them, they did have their memories. They could still perform the songs and dances of their homeland. They could hand down their customs and traditions to their children.

These enslaved men and women wanted to be free. Like people everywhere, they also wanted to express themselves. As they adapted to their new land, as they struggled to break the bonds of slavery, they took whatever chances they had to create art.

The first African Americans built their homes based on African designs. They sewed quilts and made pottery. As time passed, a few African Americans were able to earn their living

Asante-style Drum, 18th century. This drum was found in Virginia, but it was made in Africa. It was probably carried to America on a slave ship.

this way. Sign painters peddled their skills from village to village. A few graduated to painting portraits of the townsfolk.

Even after slavery ended, many white Americans did not believe African Americans could create fine art. Still, African American artists did not give up. They continued to write books, compose songs, and paint pictures.

Today, there are many famous African American artists. Very often they are **trendsetters**, taking music, literature, and film in new directions. And, like their ancestors, they celebrate their African heritage every time they make art.

CHAPTER 1

IN A NEW LAND

In 1619, a Dutch ship sailed into the harbor at Jamestown, Virginia. On board, besides the captain and crew, were 20 Africans. The ship's arrival marked the beginning of the transportation of Africans to British North America. Once the Africans left the ship, they were sold as slaves.

About 650,000, or 6.5 percent, of all African slaves ended up in British North America. These Africans came from different places. They spoke different languages and had different backgrounds, cultures, and religions.

For most of the two-month journey from Africa to America, hundreds of slaves were crowded below deck with little fresh air or space and no bedding. Only in good weather were they allowed on deck once a day.

Before slavery, Africans had reached the Americas. In fact, they may even have arrived before Christopher Columbus. More than 2,000 years ago, the Olmec people lived in what is now eastern Mexico. The giant stone heads they carved have led some researchers to believe the Olmec were descended from African explorers.

The giant stone heads carved by the Olmec people are from 5 (1.5 m) to 11 feet (3.4 m) high.

Slave traders advertised in the newspapers. This ad from the late 1700s offers slaves for sale at Ashley Ferry outside Charleston, South Carolina.

Most of the Africans brought to America as slaves came from west central Africa. There, the arts were highly developed. Though removed from their homes and cut off from their cultures, the Africans carried many of their skills to America.

African House is the oldest existing dwelling built in the United States both by and for African Americans.

In 1800, Marie Therese Coincoin, a freed slave, and her children designed and built African House on the Melrose Plantation in Natchitoches, Louisiana. The building is similar in style to straw-thatched huts found in the Congo.

Dave, a slave who was trained in setting type, began making stoneware pottery in South Carolina around 1830. Dave's pots were large and often included his name, the date, and a two-line verse. In December 2000, one of his large signed pots, dated 1853, sold for $83,600.

Pictorial Quilt, 1895–1898, by Harriet Powers. Powers may have seen some of the animals stitched into her quilt at a circus.

PHOTOGRAPH © 2006 MUSEUM OF FINE ARTS, BOSTON

Harriet Powers was born a slave in Athens, Georgia. She is known today for two quilts she created after the Civil War. The quilts pictured Bible stories as well as events from history, such as the meteor shower of 1833.

Small stoneware jugs modeled with human faces were made by slave potters in the Edgefield area of South Carolina. Similar jugs were made in parts of Africa.

The Author & the Artist

In the late 1700s, a few African Americans began to be recognized as artists and **artisans**. Phillis Wheatley was named for the slave ship, *Phillis*, which brought her to Boston, Massachusetts. Wheatley was purchased to serve as a house servant, but she was treated well by the family. Her owner's daughter even taught her to read and write. Wheatley was still a teenager when her first book of poetry was published in 1773. Colonial people found it hard to believe that an African slave could produce such fine poems. Because of this, her publisher asked Wheatley to supply a portrait of herself for the book.

When Scipio Moorhead was hired to create Wheatley's portrait, he was also a

An engraving made from Scipio Moorhead's *Portrait of Phillis Wheatley* was used as the frontispiece for her book, *Poems on Various Subjects, Religious and Moral.* Wheatley was freed the year after her book was published.

slave. He had been taught to draw and paint by the wife of his master. Moorhead made an ink drawing, *Portrait of Phillis Wheatley*, which was later **engraved** in London, England.

These lines are from a poem Phillis Wheatley wrote about Scipio Moorhead. She called it "To S.M., a Young African Painter, On Seeing His Works."

Still, wond'rous youth! each noble path pursue,

On deathless glories fix thine ardent view:

Still may the paint's and the poet's fire

To aid thy pencil, and thy verse conspire!

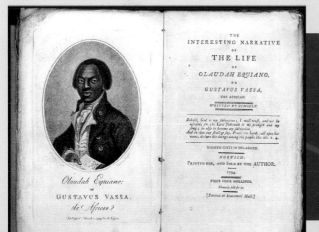

Olaudah Equiano was sold into slavery at age 11. After buying his freedom in 1766, Equiano moved to London, where he spoke out against the slave trade. In 1789, he published his autobiography, *The Interesting Narrative of the Life of Olaudah Equiano, Or Gustavus Vassa, The African.* A best-seller in England and America, the book was also translated into several languages, including German and Dutch.

Like most artists of the time, early African-American artists painted in a realistic manner. Their known works are mainly portraits of white families and, in some cases, free African Americans.

Joshua Johnston earned his living as a portrait painter in his hometown of Baltimore, Maryland. Little is known about him, except that he was born a slave and freed when he was 19 years old. Self-taught, Johnston specialized in portraits of merchants and their families. Eighty of his paintings still exist today.

Reverend G. W. Hobbs of Baltimore, Maryland, was the official artist of the

The Westwood Children, ca. 1807, by Joshua Johnston. Many of Johnston's paintings were of children. In this one, the two children on the left side are balanced by the dark wall, the window, and the small dog on the right.

Methodist Episcopal Church in the late 1700s. He was also the first African American to paint the portrait of another African American. His subject, Richard Allen, founded the first church for African Americans in Philadelphia in 1787.

Julien Hudson was a free African American who lived in New Orleans, Louisiana. From his studio on Bienville Street, he worked as a portrait painter and drawing instructor. Hudson's *Self Portrait* is the only known self-portrait painted by an African American during colonial times.

Self Portrait, 1839, by Julien Hudson. Hudson painted himself as a fashionable, well-dressed man.

Peter Bentzon is the first known African-American silversmith. After learning his craft as an **apprentice**, he opened his own shop in Philadelphia, Pennsylvania. Nine pieces have been credited to him, including this finely crafted teapot.

The first African-American landscape artists appeared in the early 1800s. Robert Scott Duncanson taught himself to draw by copying European paintings. Born in Canada, he moved to Ohio while still a young man. He began his career painting portraits. In 1848,

Blue Hole, Little Miami River, 1851, by Robert Scott Duncanson. The setting for this painting was an escape route for slaves.

Duncanson received a **commission** from Nicholas Longworth, a supporter of the arts. Duncanson was hired to paint a series of landscapes on the walls of Belmont, Longworth's mansion. Delighted with the finished work, Longworth told his friends and associates about Duncanson. Word of his ability spread, and Duncanson became known as the "best landscape painter in the West." He was one of the first African Americans to become well-known in other countries.

In 1876, *Under the Oaks*, a landscape painting by Edward Mitchell Bannister, was exhibited at the United States Centennial Exposition. This world's fair was held in Philadelphia 100 years after America became a nation. Bannister's work won a bronze medal, the top prize for painting. Bannister, a self-taught artist originally from Canada, was the first African American to win a national award. Unfortunately, the painting disappeared soon after it was sold.

Oak Trees, 1876, by Edward Mitchell Bannister. This painting is probably a lot like Bannister's lost masterpiece, *Under the Oaks*.

Edward Mitchell Bannister's landscapes were influenced by the Barbizon School, a style of painting popular in France in the mid 1800s. Barbizon School artists observed nature directly and painted outdoors, not in studios.

CHAPTER 2

UNDERGROUND ARTISTS

IN THE SWAMP.

Runaway slaves were hunted by men on horseback with dogs. If the slaves were caught, they were punished severely.

In the early 1800s, the antislavery movement began to grow. Abolitionists, people who were against slavery, joined with escaped slaves to form the Underground Railroad. It was not a real railroad but the route taken by slaves seeking freedom in the north. Along the route, abolitionists helped the runaways by providing food and safe places to hide.

Slave owners thought it was their duty to teach Africans about Christianity. Slaves were forbidden to call on their African gods or to play the drums they had always used in worship. The slaves learned about Christianity but changed it to suit their own needs. They created the songs called spirituals. The words to many spirituals, such as "Wade in the Water" and "The Gospel Train," were tied to the antislavery movement and traveling the Underground Railroad.

Harriet Tubman was an escaped slave who returned to the South to lead more than 300 slaves to freedom. She was sometimes called "Moses."

This train is bound for glory, this train. This train is bound for glory, I'm not telling you a story. This train is leaving, get on board.
—from "This Train,"
a spiritual

Harriet Tubman (1823–1913)
nurse, spy and scout

To protest slavery, many abolitionists gave out slave emblems, pictures that are meant to give moral lessons. The emblems were printed on stationery, coins, and **medallions**. Angelina E. Grimke, an abolitionist from South Carolina, commented that "Until the pictures of the slave's sufferings were drawn and held up to public gaze, no Northerner had any idea of the cruelty of the system . . . "

In 1839, Patrick Henry Reason, an African-American **printmaker** in Philadelphia, made a copper engraving of a chained slave. Above the slave are the words, "Am I not a man and a brother?" The emblem was used for an abolitionist group called the Philadelphia Vigilant Committee.

Reason had copied the slave from an earlier picture. In 1787, the noted white potter, Josiah Wedgwood, had one of his workers design a **cameo**. The cameo showed the raised profile, or side view, of a chained slave. The image became a symbol of the evils of slavery. In Reason's design, the slave faces the viewer. His eyes are cast up to heaven. By making the slave look humble and religious, Reason appealed to the viewer's emotions.

Jasper Slave Medallion, 1787, by William Hackwood

Frederick Douglass was an escaped slave who became an outspoken abolitionist. Besides giving public lectures, he wrote his autobiography, *Narrative of the Life of Frederick Douglass.*

Words of Protest

During her famous "Ain't I a Woman" speech at the 1851 Women's Convention in Akron, Ohio, Sojourner Truth said, "If the first woman God ever made was strong enough to turn the world upside down all alone, these women together ought to be able to turn it back, and get it right side up again!"

Abolitionists also used the written word to protest slavery. Sojourner Truth began life as Isabella Baumfree in Ulster County, New York. She escaped slavery in 1828 and settled in New York City. In 1843, she changed her name to Sojourner Truth and began to preach. In 1850, her memoir, *The Narrative of Sojourner Truth: A Northern Slave*, was published.

Harriet Beecher Stowe, a white woman, wrote *Uncle Tom's Cabin*. This antislavery story was published chapter by chapter in the *National Era*, a newspaper run by abolitionists. In 1852, the novel came out in book form. It sold millions of copies and encouraged thousands of people to join the antislavery cause.

In 1856, Eugene Warburg, an African-American sculptor, was inspired by Stowe's work. He carved reliefs, two-dimensional sculptures meant to be seen from the front only, that he based on the novel. The landscape painter Robert S. Duncanson painted a scene from the novel.

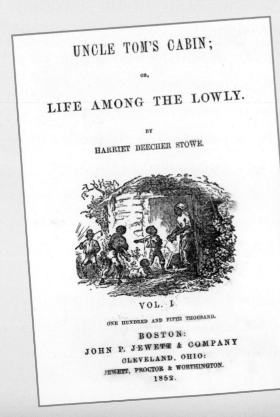

After escaping to Canada with his family, Josiah Henson returned to help other slaves find freedom. In 1849, he wrote *The Life of Josiah Henson, Formerly a Slave, Now an Inhabitant of Canada*. His life story inspired Harriet Beecher Stowe to write *Uncle Tom's Cabin*.

The title page for the first edition of Harriet Beecher Stowe's *Uncle Tom's Cabin*

CHAPTER 3

FREE AT LAST!

With slavery outlawed in 1865, African Americans were free to do a lot of things they were unable to do before. However, many white people continued to look down on them. Some formed groups that used violence. Many African Americans chose to fight this **prejudice** by staying close to home. Others took off in search of a better life.

Born in Pennsylvania, Grafton Tyler Brown was one of many African Americans who moved to the West Coast. By 1861, he worked in San Francisco as a lithographer, designing and making prints. Within five years, he owned his own shop. Among his many clients was the Wells Fargo Mining Company. Brown printed stock certificates for the company, whose

Mount Tacoma from Lake Washington, 1885, by Grafton Tyler Brown.
Mount Tacoma in the state of Washington is now known as Mount Rainier.

central image, a stagecoach, is still in use today. Brown also painted landscapes, specializing in mountain scenes.

While many American artists headed west, sculptor Edmonia Lewis chose Europe. She sailed for Florence, Italy, in 1865 to learn more about sculpture. She earned money for her trip by selling copies of busts she had made of Robert Gould Shaw. Colonel Shaw, a white man, led a unit of black troops in the Civil War. Lewis was unusual among artists of her day because she used African Americans and Native Americans as her subjects.

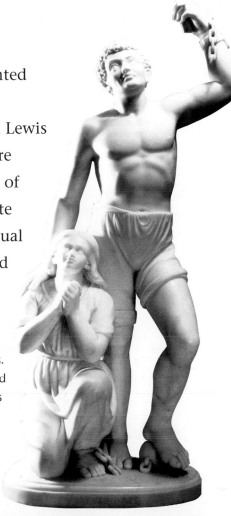

Forever Free, 1867, by Edmonia lewis. The glad expressions and broken chain in Lewis's sculpture celebrate the Emancipation Proclamation that freed the slaves.

A former slave, Booker T. Washington (above left) founded the Tuskegee Institute, a school for African Americans. George Washington Carver, a teacher at Tuskegee, wrote poetry and painted, but he is best known as a scientist. His research on peanuts resulted in the creation of more than 300 products.

In 1893, *The Banjo Lesson*, a **genre** painting by Henry Ossawa Tanner, was exhibited at a gallery in Philadelphia. The artist was pleased with the praise his first important painting won from critics. Unfortunately, genre paintings were not valued as much as art that pictured classical or historical scenes. Tanner began to paint biblical scenes. *The Annunciation* was unusual for its use of true-to-life details. Unlike other religious paintings of its time, it shows its subject, Mary, the future mother of Jesus, as a poor peasant woman.

The Banjo Lesson, 1893, by Henry Ossawa Tanner. The banjo was invented by African Americans.

Ragtime, a lively new kind of music, became popular in the late 1800s. Scott Joplin traveled around the country, singing and playing the **cornet** and piano. He became one of the most famous ragtime composers. The first ragtime song he wrote, "Maple Leaf Rag," was published in 1899. Soon after his death in 1917, interest in ragtime died down as jazz took over. In the 1970s, Joplin's "The Entertainer" was used as the theme song of the movie *The Sting*. This sparked a new interest in ragtime and in Joplin's music.

Scott Joplin received a penny for each copy of "Maple Leaf Rag" sheet music that was sold.

CHAPTER 4

A NEW CENTURY

Lift every voice and sing Till earth and heaven ring, Ring with the harmonies of Liberty.

—James Weldon Johnson, from "Lift Every Voice and Sing"

The new century brought great change for all Americans. Cities sprang up, populated with newly arrived immigrants from Europe. Instead of working on farms, more and more people toiled in factories. New inventions also changed the way people lived. In 1903, Orville Wright flew the first airplane. Model T cars rolled off the assembly line. In this new world, African Americans looked to make their mark.

James Weldon Johnson was a man who wore many hats. During his lifetime he was a songwriter, poet, novelist, and journalist. In 1900, he wrote the words for "Lift Every Voice and Sing." It is often called "the Negro National Anthem." Johnson wrote these lyrics to celebrate Abraham Lincoln's birthday.

Augusta Fells Savage was an African-American sculptor who worked in New York. In 1939, she created *The Harp*, a huge sculpture inspired by Johnson's poem. Commissioned by the New York World's Fair, the work is a 16-foot- (4.9-m-) tall harp whose strings are singing children.

Augusta Fells Savage in her studio working on *The Harp*, ca. 1937. Small metal copies of Savage's sculpture were sold as souvenirs at the 1939 World's Fair.

A leading African American, W. E. B. DuBois was both a scholar and an activist. In 1909, he helped found the National Association for the Advancement of Colored People (NAACP). It remains an important civil rights organization to this day. DuBois also edited the NAACP's magazine, *The Crisis*.

From 1913 to 1946, hundreds of thousands of African Americans moved from the rural South to the urban cities of the North. They hoped for better jobs and a brighter future. This movement came to be called the Great Migration. It set the scene for the cultural period known as the Harlem **Renaissance**.

Meta Vaux Warrick Fuller was one of the first African Americans to use African themes and folk tales for her sculptures. After graduating from the Pennsylvania School of Industrial Arts, Fuller went to Paris, France, to continue her studies. There she met Auguste Rodin, a leading white sculptor. When he saw her work, he said, "My child, you are a born sculptor, you have a sense of form!"

The blues, a style of music that came out of the songs of Southern blacks, can be traced back as far as the 1860s. Around 1910, it became extremely popular through the publication of W. C. Handy's "Memphis Blues" and "St. Louis Blues." With "Crazy Blues" in 1920, Mamie Smith became the first singer to record a blues song.

The Awakening of Ethiopia, ca. 1910, by Meta Vaux Warrick Fuller. The woman portrayed in Fuller's statue represents Africa.

The cover of the 1920 sheet music for "Crazy Blues" shows Mamie Smith and her band, the Jazz Hounds.

CRAZY BLUES

By PERRY BRADFORD

MAMIE SMITH AND HER JAZZ HOUNDS

Get this number for your phonograph on Okeh Record No. 4169

PUBLISHED BY
PERRY BRADFORD
MUSIC PUB CO
1547 BROADWAY, N. Y. C.

When 32 men were trapped after an explosion in an underground tunnel, Garrett Morgan's invention, the gas mask, helped to save their lives. Later, it was used in World War I. This African-American inventor also came up with the idea for the traffic signal.

I of the dark eyes
And crinkly hair . . .
I am America seeking the stars . . .
—Langston Hughes, from "America"

From about 1920 to the mid 1930s, there was a great flowering of activity by African Americans in the fields of art, literature, and music. This period came to be called the Harlem Renaissance. It was named after Harlem, an African-American neighborhood in New York City, which was then the center of African-American culture.

During this time, African-American artists such as author Zora Neale Hurston set out to express their lives as black Americans. As a child, Hurston lived in Eatonville, Florida, an African-American town. It became the setting for many of her books, including her best-known work, *Their Eyes Were Watching God*.

Forgotten for many years, Zora Neale Hurston's books were rediscovered and reprinted in the 1970s. They are still in print today.

One of the leaders of the Harlem Renaissance was Alain Locke, a professor at Howard University. Locke encouraged African-American artists to look to Africa for **inspiration**. In 1925, he edited *The New Negro: An Interpretation*. The book was a collection of essays by African Americans focusing on Harlem. It was illustrated by Aaron Douglas. Douglas also illustrated books for leading African-American authors. Among them were Countee Cullen, a novelist, and Langston Hughes, a poet.

Rebirth, ca. 1925, by Aaron Douglas.
This is one of the ten drawings that Douglas created for a book called *The New Negro*.

James Van Der Zee owned a photography studio in Harlem. Besides doing portraits, he took photographs of parades, weddings, funerals, and people out for a night on the town.

Couple in Raccoon Coats, 1932

HOT JAZZ!

Jazz Singers, ca. 1934, by Archibald J. Motley, Jr. Motley captured the rhythms of the music in this and other paintings.

Jazz, with its roots in African, French, and American music, came into its own during the Harlem Renaissance. Like many other artists, Archibald J. Motley, Jr., was caught up in the excitement of the time. He lived and worked in Chicago, where he painted lively, colorful scenes of urban African Americans enjoying life.

Hip hip, the joint is jumpin'

It's really jumpin'

Come in, cats, and shake your hats,

I mean this joint is jumpin'!

These words, which were recorded by Fats Waller, described the jazz clubs of the 1920s and '30s. In 1934, the Apollo Theater in Harlem started to feature up-and-coming new artists. Many famous musicians got their start on Amateur Night at the Apollo. Ella Fitzgerald was one of the first, beginning a singing career that would last more than 60 years.

Duke Ellington and his band brought a new level of style and elegance to jazz. They played all over New York City, but it was radio broadcasts from the Cotton Club that made them famous throughout America in the late 1920s.

Aspects of Negro Life:
The Negro in an African Setting,
1934, by Aaron Douglas.
In his mural, Douglas used a
limited range of color and painted
silhouettes of people against an
abstract background.

In 1929, the Great Depression began. Millions of people were out of work. To help Americans, President Franklin Delano Roosevelt launched a set of programs called the New Deal. The programs created jobs, as well as gave money to those in need. One program was of special help to artists. Known as the WPA (Work Projects Administration), it hired about 10,000 artists to produce public works of art.

Many artists working for the WPA were commissioned to paint murals. They decorated banks, bus stations, post offices, and schools. Aaron Douglas created four murals called *Aspects of Negro Life*. They traced African Americans from their origins in Africa, through slavery, emancipation, and the Great Migration. The murals were installed at the 135th Street branch of the New York Public Library.

While working on WPA projects, the painter William Johnson learned silkscreening, a way of making prints using stencils and ink. He created many colorful prints using this medium. Although he had studied art, Johnston liked to work in a primitive style. His art featured simple forms and shapes and bold colors.

Going to Church, ca. 1940–1941, by William Johnson. Johnson produced several versions of this work in different media. This one was painted with oils on burlap.

Paul Williams is considered by many people to be the first African-American architect. He designed more than 2,000 homes. Some of the public buildings and projects he worked on are the Los Angeles County Court House, the Los Angeles International Airport (left), and the United Nations building in Paris, France.

Defense Worker, ca. 1942, by Dox Thrash. Thrash was a printmaker who worked for the WPA in Philadelphia. He made this print of an African American working at a defense plant.

On December 7, 1941, the Japanese bombed Pearl Harbor in Hawaii. Americans prepared for war. In Europe, World War II had already started. America helped out by making weapons for Great Britain and the Soviet Union. New jobs were created, and the Great Depression ended. Before 1941, factories did not hire African Americans. Then, President Roosevelt ruled that African Americans must be allowed to work in defense plants.

Jacob Lawrence, a student of the Harlem Art Workshop, learned all he could about African art and history. He also studied the work of African-American artists of the day. His interest in history and culture shows in his work. He painted a series of 60 panels called *The Migration of the Negro*. The style of this work is similar to that found in folk art.

Both a printmaker and a sculptor, Elizabeth Catlett used her art to bring about social change. After graduating from the University of Iowa with a degree in sculpture, Catlett traveled to Mexico City. There she studied painting, sculpture, and lithography. She liked Mexico so much that she stayed, eventually becoming a Mexican citizen.

The Migration of the Negro, Panel no. 1, 1940–1941, by Jacob Lawrence. Lawrence's paintings of the Great Migration were based on his family's history.

African Americans were making great strides in the arts, but this wasn't the case in other fields. As of 1946, no major league sports team had an African American on its payroll. That changed the following year when Jackie Robinson played his first game as a Brooklyn Dodger. Just two years later, he was named the National League's Most Valuable Player.

CHAPTER 5

DARING TO
DREAM

After World War II, abstract art, which had started in Europe, caught on in the United States. Like other artists, African Americans such as Norman Lewis were eager to try their hand at this new form of art. Abstract artists did not try to portray a subject exactly as it appeared. They were more interested in form and color and in expressing themselves through the act of creating.

In the 1950s, African Americans, tired of being **discriminated** against, began to demand equal rights. In the South, African Americans and whites were educated in separate public schools. In 1954, the Supreme Court ruled that such **segregation** was unconstitutional. The following year in Alabama, Rosa Parks, an African-American seamstress, refused to give up her seat on a bus to a white man. Her arrest sparked the Montgomery Bus Boycott. For a year, African Americans in

Rosa Parks being fingerprinted after her arrest.

Montgomery refused to ride the buses. The boycott ended when the Supreme Court ruled in favor of the strikers.

Though Marian Anderson was a world-famous concert singer, she was prevented from singing at Constitution Hall in Washington, D.C., in 1939. Outraged fans protested, and the concert was rescheduled outdoors at the Lincoln Memorial. More than 75,000 people attended.

In 1955, Marian Anderson became the first African American to sing with the Metropolitan Opera in New York City.

Alvin Ailey began his career with the first racially mixed dance company in the United States. In 1958, he founded the Alvin Ailey American Dance Theater. One of Ailey's goals as a choreographer was to enrich American modern dance. He arranged some 79 ballets before his death in 1989.

> I have a dream that my four children will one day live in a nation where they will not be judged by the color of their skin but by the content of their character.
>
> —Martin Luther King, Jr.

The 1960s were a time of great change for Americans. Young people marched on the nation's streets and campuses to protest the war in Vietnam. The Civil Rights movement, which had simmered in the 1950s, came to a full boil. Martin Luther King, Jr., the movement's leader, encouraged African Americans to demand equal rights without using violence. During the March on Washington in 1963, King gave his inspiring speech, "I Have a Dream." Sadly, this peace-loving man was **assassinated** in 1968.

Betye Saar of Los Angeles, California, is interested in exploring racial **stereotypes**. One of her most famous works is *The Liberation of Aunt Jemima*. An advertising image, Aunt Jemima appeared on boxes of pancake batter. Saar turned the image of a smiling African-American servant on its head. Her version of Aunt Jemima carries a broom in one hand and a rifle in the other.

Freedom Now, 1965, by Reginald Gammon. Gammon used a photograph of the March on Washington as a basis for his painting.

The Block (Detail), 1971, by Romare Bearden. Bearden's lively collage is a celebration of a neighborhood in Harlem. The entire six-panel collage is 18 feet (5.5 m) long.

Romare Bearden was primarily a painter until the 1960s, when he became interested in **collage**. His early collages combined clippings from newspapers and magazines with pencil or ink line drawings. Bearden then enlarged some of these collages with a photostat machine. In 1964, his work, entitled *Projections*, was exhibited at a New York gallery, where it was a big success.

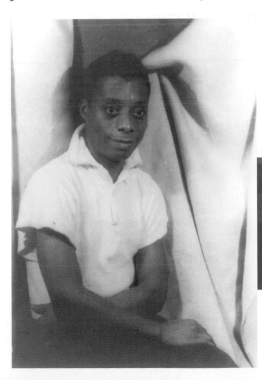

After living in Europe for nearly 20 years, author James Baldwin returned to the United States in 1957 to work in the Civil Rights Movement. His 1963 book, *The Fire Next Time*, was a powerful plea for whites and African-Americans to work together to end racial injustice.

Tar Beach, 1988, by Faith Ringgold. In 1991, Ringgold published a children's book based on this quilt. Like the painting, it is called *Tar Beach*.

Today's African-American artists are proud of their rich heritage. Some pay tribute to African-American leaders. Barbara Chase-Riboud is one such artist. She made four sculptures in honor of Malcolm X, a civil rights leader of the 1960s who was assassinated. Other artists, like Faith Ringgold, adapt traditional crafts, such as story quilting, to create new art forms.

Jean-Michel Basquiat was inspired by the graffiti he saw scrawled on walls and subway cars in New York City. His "paintings" are a hodgepodge of found objects, doodles, and printed words, mingling with historical figures, comic book characters, and medical illustrations.

Spike Lee was one of the first African-American filmmakers to gain a wide following. His movies, such as *Do the Right Thing* and *Malcolm X*, portray racial issues from an African-American viewpoint.

Oprah Winfrey made television history when *The Oprah Winfrey Show* became the highest-rated talk show ever broadcast. In 1996, she started a book club on her show, which made many **literary** books into best-sellers. In 2004, Winfrey was listed in *Time* magazine's 100 Most Influential People in the World.

In 2004, Oprah Winfrey was named Favorite Talk Show Host at the 30th Annual People's Choice Awards.

In 1970, Toni Morrison published *The Bluest Eye*. Like her later novels, it is concerned with the experiences of African Americans, especially black women. Morrison grew up in Ohio, where her family shared songs and folktales, giving her a strong appreciation for black culture. In 1993, Toni Morrison became the first African American to be awarded the Nobel Prize for Literature.

1619 The first Africans are brought to Jamestown to be sold as slaves

1745 Olaudah Equiano born (d. 1801)

ca. 1750 Scipio Moorhead born (d. after 1773)

ca. 1753 Phillis Wheatley born (d. 1784)

ca. 1765 Joshua Johnson born (d. 1830)

ca. 1780 Reverend G. W. Hobbs born (d. after 1850)

ca. 1783 Peter Bentzon born (d. ?)

1789 Josiah Henson born (d. 1883)

ca. 1797 Sojourner Truth born (d. 1883)

1800 Marie Therese Coincoin builds African House

1805 Angelina E. Grimke born (d.1879)

1811 Harriet Beecher Stowe born (d. 1896)

1817 Patrick Henry Reason born (d. ca. 1850);
Frederick Douglass born (d. 1895)

ca. 1820 Harriet Tubman born (d. 1913)

1821 Robert Scott Duncanson born (d. 1872)

1825 Eugene Warburg born (d. 1867)

1828 Edward Mitchell Bannister born (d.1901)

1837 Harriet Powers born (d. 1911)

1841 Grafton Tyler Brown born (d. 1918)

1843 Edmonia Lewis born (d. 1911)

1856 Booker T. Washington born (d. 1919)

1859 Henry Ossawa Tanner born (d. 1937)

1861 Civil War begins (ends 1865)

ca. 1864 George Washington Carver born (d. 1943)

1868 Scott Joplin born (d. 1917); W. E. B. DuBois born (d. 1963)

1871 James Weldon Johnson born (d. 1938)

1873 W. C. Handy born (d. 1958)

1877 Meta Vaux Warrick Fuller born (d. 1968);
Garrett Morgan born (d. 1963)

1883 Mamie Smith born (d. 1946)

1886 Alain Locke born (d. 1954); James Van der Zee born (d. 1983)

1891 Zora Neale Hurston born (d. 1960);
Archibald J. Motley, Jr., born (d. 1981)

1893 Dox Thrash born (d. 1965)

1894 Paul Williams born (d. 1980)

1897 Marian Anderson born (d. 1993)

1899 Duke Ellington born (d. 1974); Aaron Douglas born (d. 1979)

1900 Augusta Fells Savage born (d. 1962)

1901 William Johnston born (d. 1970)

1902 Langston Hughes born (d. 1967)

1903 Countee Cullen born (d. 1946)

1904 Fats Waller born (d. 1943)

1911 Romare Bearden born (d. 1988)

1913 Great Migration begins (ends 1946); Rosa Parks born

1915 Elizabeth Catlett born

1917 Jacob Lawrence born (d. 2000)

1918 Ella Fitzgerald born (d. 1996)

1919 Jackie Robinson born (d. 1972)

ca. 1920 Harlem Renaissance begins (ends mid 1930s)

1921 Reginald Gammon born

1924 James Baldwin born (d. 1987)

1925 Malcolm X born (d. 1965)

1926 Betye Saar born

1929 Great Depression begins (ends 1940);
Martin Luther King, Jr., born (d. 1968)

1931 Alvin Ailey born (d. 1989); Toni Morrison born

1934 Faith Ringgold born

1939 World War II begins (ends 1945); Barbara Chase-Riboud born

1944 Judith Jamison born

1954 Oprah Winfrey born

1955 Montgomery Bus Boycott takes place

1957 Spike Lee born

1960 Jean-Michel Basquiat born (d. 1988)

1963 During the March on Washington,
Martin Luther King, Jr., delivers "I Have a Dream" speech

artisan craftsperson

assassinate to murder, usually for political reasons

cameo a small relief carving, usually of a person in profile

collage a work of art made from different kinds of materials, such as cut paper, bits of cloth, photographs, newspaper or magazine clippings, and foil

commission a job; also to hire someone to do a certain job

cornet a musical instrument that looks and sounds much like a trumpet

discriminate to treat people differently because of their race, gender, or religion

engrave to cut letters, designs, or pictures into blocks or plates in order to make a print, which is called an engraving

genre a type of painting in which the picture portrays events or scenes from everyday life

inspiration something that awakens an emotional or mental response, sparking a burst of creativity

literary of or relating to books, especially serious books of fiction or nonfiction

medallion a large medal or a tablet showing a picture in relief

prejudice an unfounded and unfriendly belief about people based on their race, gender, or religion

printmaker an artist who designs and creates original prints

renaissance a period marked by a flowering of the arts

segregation a separation of people based on their race, gender, or religion

stereotype a belief that all members of a certain race, gender, or religion act or look alike

trendsetter someone who sets a new style

Tonya Bolden, *Wake Up Your Souls: A Celebration of African American Artists*, Harry N. Abrams, Inc., 2003

Michael L. Cooper, *Slave Spirituals and the Jubilee Singers*, Houghton Mifflin, 2001

Virginia Hamilton, *The People Could Fly: American Black Folktales*, Knopf, 1993

Laban Carrick Hill, *Harlem Stomp! A Cultural History of the Harlem Renaissance*, Little, Brown & Company, 2004

Jacob Lawrence, *The Great Migration: An American Story*, HarperCollins Children's Books, 1995

Julius Lester, *To Be a Slave*, Penguin Putnam, 2000

Mary E. Lyons, *Stitching Stars: The Story Quilts of Harriet Powers*, Simon & Schuster, 1993

Walter Dean Myers, *One More River to Cross: An African American Photograph Album*, Harcourt, 1999

Belinda Rochelle, *Words with Wings: A Treasury of African-American Poetry and Art*, William Morrow, 2000

Web Sites

Judy Chicago's *The Dinner Party*—
Famous Female Activists and Artists
www.english.ilstu.edu/351/hypertext98/hankins/african/african.html

PBS: African-American World
Arts and Culture
www.pbs.org/wnet/aaworld/arts/spotlight.html

Harlem 1900–1940: An African-American Community
The Schomburg Center for Black Research in Black Culture
The New York Public Library
www.si.umich.edu/CHICO/Harlem

ACKNOWLEDGMENTS

The editors wish to thank the following organizations and individuals for permission to reprint the literary quotes and to reproduce the images in this book. Every effort has been made to obtain permission from the owners of all materials. Any errors that may have been made are unintentional and will be corrected in future printings if notice is given to the publisher.

Cover, p. 9 (top): Harriet Powers, American, 1837–1911/*Pictorial quilt*/American (Athens, Georgia), 1895–98/Pieced, appliquéd, and embroidered printed cotton/175 x 266.7 cm (68 7/8 x 105 in.)/Museum of Fine Arts, Boston/Bequest of Maxim Karolik/ 64.619
Title page, p. 32: Archibald J. Motley, Jr. (African-American; 1891–1981)/"The Jazz Singers"/oil on canvas; c. 1934/32 1/8" h. x 42 1/4" w./Provenance: W. P. A.; 1934/Permanent Collection—Western Illinois University Art Gallery/Courtesy Western Illinois University Art Gallery, Macomb, Illinois
p. 5: *Asante-style drum*/African, 18th century AD/Height: 40 cm/From Virginia, southeastern North America/© The Trustees of The British Museum
p. 6: The Africans of the slave bark *Wildfire*/ Library of Congress
p. 7 (top): Stone head of Olmec ruler in helmet, ca. 1200 B.C.E./Height: 9 ft, weight: 20 tons/La Venta, Tabasco, Mexico/The Art Archive/Mireille Vautier; **(bottom):** Newspaper ad for slave sale at Ashley Ferry, South Carolina, 1780s/Library of Congress
p. 8: African House/Library of Congress
p. 9 (bottom): *Face Vessels*/Alkaline-glazed stoneware/ Attributed to Black slave potters/Edgefield District, South Carolina/Mid-19th century/5" high x 3" wide/Catalog numbers 324313 and 324314/Smithsonian Institution/National Museum of American History
p. 10: Frontispiece from *Poems on Various Subjects, Religious and Moral* by Phillis Wheatley, 1773, Scipio Moorhead/Library of Congress
p. 11: Frontispiece and title page from *The Interesting Narrative of the Life of Olaudah Equiano*, 1794/ Library of Congress
p. 12: Joshua Johnson/*The Westwood Children*, c. 1807, oil on canvas/Gift of Edgar William and Bernice Chrysler Garbisch/1959.11.1.(1536)/PA/Image © 2005 Board of Trustees, National Gallery of Art, Washington, DC
p. 13 (top): *Self Portrait* by Julien Hudson, on canvas, 1839/Collection of the Louisiana State Museum/LSM # 07526 B/; **(bottom):** Peter Bentzon/Teapot, ca. 1817/The Saint Louis Art Museum/Museum Minority Artists Purchase Fund and funds given by The Equal Sweetener Foundation and the Paul and Elissa Cahn Foundation
p. 14: Robert S. Duncanson, *Blue Hole, Little Miami River*/Cincinnati Art Museum, Gift of Norbert Heerman and Arthur Helbig/1926.18
p. 15: Edward Mitchell Bannister (1828–1901). *Oak Trees*, 1876. Oil on canvas, 33 7/8 x 60 1/4 in./Smithsonian American Art Museum, Washington, DC/Art Resource, NY
p. 16: *In the Swamp*/Library of Congress
p. 17: Harriet Tubman/Library of Congress
p. 18: Wood engraving of Angelina Grimke/ Library of Congress
p. 19 (top): Wedgwood black on yellow Jasper Slave Medallion (1787), William Hackwood/By courtesy of the Wedgwood Museum Trust, Staffordshire, England; **(bottom):** Frederick Douglass/Library of Congress

p. 20: Sojourner Truth/Library of Congress
p. 21 (top): Reverend Josiah Henson, 1789-1883/The Art Archive/Private Collection; **(bottom):** Frontispiece for first edition of *Uncle Tom's Cabin* by Harriet Beecher Stowe, 1852/The Art Archive/Culver Pictures
p. 22: Grafton Tyler Brown, *Mount Tacoma from Lake Washington*, 1885/Courtesy of Braarud Fine Art, LaConner, WA
p. 23 (right): Edmonia Lewis, *Forever Free*/Marble/1867/ Howard University Gallery of Art, Washington, DC; **(left):** Booker T. Washington/Library of Congress
p. 24: Henry Ossawa Tanner, *The Banjo Lesson* (1893)/ Hampton University Museum, Hampton, Virginia
p. 25 (top): Cover of Scott Joplin's "Maple Leaf Rag"/The Lester S. Levy Collection of Sheet Music, The Sheridan Libraries of The Johns Hopkins University
p. 26: "Lift Every Voice and Sing," from SAINT PETER RELATES AN INCIDENT by James Weldon Johnson, copyright 1917, 1921, 1935 by James Weldon Johnson, copyright renewed © 1963 by Grace Nail Johnson. Used by permission of Viking Penguin, a division of Penguin Group (USA) Inc.
p. 27 (right): Augusta Savage in her studio working on *The Harp*, ca. 1937/Photograph © Morgan and Marvin Smith/Photographs and Prints Division, Schomburg Center for Research in Black Culture, The New York Public Library, Astor, Lenox and Tilden Foundations (SC-CN-94-0174); **(left):** W. E. B. DuBois/Library of Congress
p. 28: Meta Warrick Fuller. *The Awakening of Ethiopia.* [sculpture], ca. 1910/Art & Artifacts Division, Schomburg Center for Research in Black Culture, The New York Public Library, Astor, Lenox and Tilden Foundations
p. 29 (right): "Crazy Blues" Sheet Music/From the Collections of The Henry Ford (99.153.1/G5985); **(left):** Garrett Morgan wearing his gas mask/The Western Reserve Historical Society, Cleveland, Ohio (PG 246)
p. 30: Excerpt from THE COLLECTED POEMS OF LANGSTON HUGHES by Langston Hughes, copyright © 1994 by The Estate of Langston Hughes. Used by permission of Alfred A. Knopf, a division of Random House, Inc.; Photograph of Zora Neale Hurston by Carl Van Vechten/Library of Congress
p. 31 (top): Aaron Douglas, *Rebirth*, ca. 1925, ink and graphite on paper/Howard University Gallery of Art, Washington, DC; **(bottom):** *Couple in Raccoon Coats*, 1932/Photographer: James VanDerZee/© Donna Mussenden VanDerZee
p. 33: "The Joint Is Jumpin'" from AIN'T MISBEHAVIN'/ Words by Andy Razaf and J. C. Johnson/Music by Thomas "Fats" Waller/© 1938 PHILIP L. PONCE, INC./© Renewed 1966 EDWIN H. MORRIS & COMPANY, A Division of MPL Music Publishing, Inc., CHAPPELL & CO., RAZAF MUSIC CO. and RECORD MUSIC CO. All Rights Reserved; Portrait of Duke Ellington wearing top hat, ca. 1940s (ps_mus_cd10_133)/Music Division, The New York Public Library for the Performing Arts, Astor, Lenox and Tilden Foundations

p. 34: Aaron Douglas. *Aspects of Negro Life: The Negro in an African Setting.* 1934. Oil on canvas/Art & Artifacts Division, Schomburg Center for Research in Black Culture, The New York Public Library, Astor, Lenox and Tilden Foundations
p. 35 (top): William H. Johnson (1901–1970) © Copyright. Going to Church, ca. 1940–1941. Oil on burlap, 38 1/8 x 45 1/2 in./Smithsonian American Art Museum, Washington, DC/Art Resource, NY; **(bottom):** Los Angeles International Airport/Jeff Grace/ LA Opinion Photos/Newscom
p. 36: Dox Thrash, *Defense Worker*, c. 1941/Federal Works Agency, Work Projects Administration, on deposit at the Philadelphia Museum of Art, 1943/2-1943-275(18)
p. 37 (top): Jacob Lawrence, *The Migration of the Negro Panel no. 1*/1940–1941/Casein tempera on hardboard/12 x 18 in./30.48 x 45.72 cm/Acquired 1942/The Phillips Collection, Washington, DC/© 2005 The Estate of Gwendolyn Knight Lawrence/Artists Rights Society (ARS), New York; **(bottom):** Jackie Robinson/Library of Congress
p. 38: Rosa Parks being fingerprinted in Montgomery, AL/Library of Congress
p. 39 (top): Photograph of Marian Anderson by Carl Van Vechten/Library of Congress; **(bottom):** Portrait of Alvin Ailey. n.d. (ps_dan_cd3_37)/Jerome Robbins Dance Division, The New York Public Library for the Performing Arts, Astor, Lenox and Tilden Foundations
p. 40: Excerpt from "I Have a Dream" by Martin Luther King, Jr./Courtesy of The King Estate; Reginald Gammon, *Freedom Now*, 1965/Acrylic on board/Courtesy National Afro-American Museum and Cultural Center, Wilberforce, Ohio/Art copyright © Reginald Gammon
p. 41 (top): Romare Bearden (American, 1911–1988), *The Block*, 1971 (Detail). Cut and pasted printed, colored and metallic papers, photostats, pencil, ink marker, gouache, watercolor, and pen and ink on Masonite; Overall: 48 x 216 in. (121.9 x 548.6 cm); six panels, each 48 x 36 in. (121.9 x 91.4 cm)/The Metropolitan Museum of Art, Gift of Mr. and Mrs. Samuel Shore, 1978 (1978.61.1–3) Photograph copyright © 1992 The Metropolitan Museum of Art/Art © Romare Bearden Foundation/Licensed by VAGA, New York, NY; **(bottom):** Photograph of James Baldwin by Carl Van Vechten/ Library of Congress
p. 42: Faith Ringgold/*Tar Beach*, 1988/Acrylic paint on canvas bordered with printed, painted, quilted and pieced cloth/189.5 x 174 cm (74 5/8 x 68 1/2 inches)/Solomon R. Guggenheim Museum, New York/Gift, Mr. and Mrs. Gus and Judith Lieber, 1988/88.3620/Photograph by David Heald/© The Solomon R. Guggenheim Foundation, New York/Art: Faith Ringgold © 1988
p. 43 (top): Oprah Winfrey/Lisa O'Connor/Zuma Press/Newscom; **(bottom):** Toni Morrison/Nancy Kaszerman/Zuma Press/Newscom
Backgrounds, pp. 4–5, 25, 26, 29 (trumpet), **and all sidebar backgrounds:** Ablestock